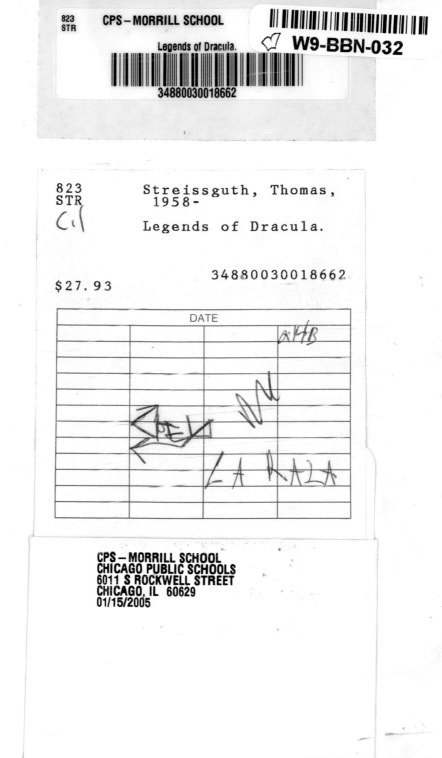

1. Vampir (Vampirus spectrum). ¼.
(Art. *Fledermäuse.*)

2. Kopf des Vampirs.

3. Kopf der Zwergfledermaus.
(Vesperugo pipistrellus.)

4. Kopf der Hufeisen
(Rhinolophus ferrum equ

5

Legends of

DRACULA

Tom Streissguth

Lerner Publications Company
Minneapolis

Lerner Publications Company
241 First Avenue North
Minneapolis, MN 55401

Website address: www.lernerbooks.com

Library of Congress Cataloging-in-Publication Data

Streissguth, Thomas, 1958–
    Legends of Dracula / Tom Streissguth.
        p.   cm. — (A & E biography)
    Includes bibliographical references and index.
    Summary: Discusses Vlad the Impaler, the historical person behind Count Dracula, describes how Bram Stoker came to write his famous novel about him, and examines how the character has been portrayed on stage and screen.
    ISBN 0–8225–4942–5 (alk. paper)
    1. Stoker, Bram, 1847–1912. Dracula—Juvenile literature.
2. Horror tales, English—History and criticism—Juvenile literature. 3. Vlad III, Prince of Wallachia, 1430 or 31–1476 or 7—Juvenile literature. 4. Dracula, Count (Fictitious character)—Juvenile literature. 5. Wallachia—Kings and rulers—Biography—Juvenile literature. 6. Stoker, Bram, 1847–1912—Adaptations—Juvenile literature. 7. Horror tales, English—Adaptations—Juvenile literature. 8. Vampires in literature—Juvenile literature. 9. Vampires—Romania—Juvenile literature. [1. Vlad III, Prince of Wallachia, 1430 or 31–1476 or 7. 2. Kings, queens, rulers, etc. 3. Stoker, Bram, 1847–1912. Dracula. 4. Horror stories—History and criticism. 5. Dracula, Count (Fictitious character) 6. Vampires.] I. Title. II. Series.
PR6037.T617D7   1999
823'.8—DC21   98-8428

Manufactured in the United States of America
1 2 3 4 5 6 – JR – 04 03 02 01 00 99

CONTENTS

Introduction............................6

Part I *Vlad the Impaler*

1 The Valley of Corpses 9
2 Son of the Dragon.......................15
3 The Impaler 27

Part II *Bram Stoker's Dracula*

4 Vampires 41
5 Bram Stoker...........................53
6 Bram Stoker's Dracula..................63
7 The Book of the Undead 77

Part III *Dracula on Stage and Screen*

8 Vampire Shows 83
9 Dracula in Hollywood 95
10 The Modern Dracula 101

Sources...............................106
Bibliography 107
Filmography..........................108
Index 109
Pronunciation Guide 111

INTRODUCTION

FOR MORE THAN ONE HUNDRED YEARS, COUNT Dracula has been scaring readers and moviegoers all over the world. The Count can hypnotize you with words, with a look, or even with a creepy smile. He can turn himself into a bat, a wolf, a large dog, or a sinister cloud of mist. He stands tall in fine evening clothes and wears a long black cape. He died a long time ago—now he walks at night and wants to drink your blood. There are a few things he can't stand: daylight, the sight of a crucifix, and the smell of garlic. He is a vampire.

The character of Dracula first materialized in 1897, when an Irish writer named Bram Stoker published the novel *Dracula, or the Undead*. To write the story, Stoker spent seven years studying travel and history books that described Transylvania, Wallachia, and the Carpathian Mountains in Central Europe. Stoker also learned about a historical prince who once lived in that mysterious region. This prince, named Dracula, was commissioned by the pope to defend the realm of the church against non-Christian invaders. But Dracula had a nasty reputation as a tyrant who tortured and murdered his own subjects as well as his enemies. Stoker decided to use Prince Dracula as the model for his fictional vampire.

In the years since Bram Stoker's *Dracula* was first published, hundreds of books and movies have borrowed its characters and plot. The most famous of these works was the 1931 movie *Dracula* starring Bela Lugosi as the Count. Audiences loved the Count's weird, staring expression, strange accent, and dark, menacing eyes. But as you are about to discover, the deeds committed by the real Prince Dracula were just as bloody and frightening as those committed by the Dracula of supernatural make-believe.

The true Dracula was a holy knight of the church . . . a charismatic, heroic crusader who, in the 1400s, saved his Christian homeland from invasion by Moslem Turks.

> —James V. Hart, screenwriter of
> *Bram Stoker's Dracula*

The historical Dracula, Vlad the Impaler, was a monumentally wicked man and . . . reading about him can make one very uncomfortable.

> —Leonard Wolf, author of
> *Dracula: The Connoisseur's Guide*

PART I

VLAD THE
IMPALER

Chapter **ONE**

THE VALLEY OF CORPSES

IT WAS THE SUMMER OF **1462.** THE SUN BURNED down on the plains and river valleys of Wallachia, a land on the Balkan peninsula of Europe. Mohammed II, sultan (ruler) of the powerful Ottoman Empire, was leading his army of Turkish and Bulgarian soldiers toward the steep mountains that separated Wallachia from Transylvania—the "land beyond the forest." Mohammed's enemy, the Wallachian prince Vlad III, was retreating through the high mountain passes. Soon, the sultan was sure, this campaign and his opponent would be finished. Wallachia would be conquered and once again made into an obedient Turkish province. Mohammed would capture and behead this arrogant, treacherous prince and return in triumph to his palace in Istanbul, the capital of the Ottoman Empire.

The sultan's army easily captured Tirgoviste, capital city of Wallachia. But the Wallachian army had abandoned the town. The treasures of the church and of the prince's palace were gone. There was no food in the shops or in the homes of the townspeople. Livestock had disappeared; crops in the surrounding fields had been burnt to black stubble. The Turks could find no water to drink, except for the poisoned water that filled the city's wells. Although Mohammed's army was growing hungry and weak in the scorching summer heat, the sultan pushed on.

A few miles north of Tirgoviste, the Ottoman army came to a narrow valley. A strange silence descended as a terrifying scene appeared. These soldiers had seen many bloody and violent sights, but nothing like this. High above them, pierced by tall wooden stakes, hung a silent army of bodies. The corpses had been dangling there for many weeks, impaled like human shish kebabs. Mohammed's soldiers gazed in horror at the twenty thousand bodies, half eaten by birds and rotting in the sun.

Mohammed ordered his army past the gruesome valley of corpses. That night, he told his men to raise mounds of earth around the camp and post extra guards to watch for the enemy. He then retired to his tent to consider his plans. Should he follow Vlad into the hills and forests of Transylvania? He would have to cross the high

Carpathian Mountains to follow the Wallachians; he would have to find food and fresh water; his army would lose many men to disease, hunger, and ambush.

Mohammed was renowned throughout Europe for his military skill and bravery. Nine years earlier, he had conquered Constantinople, the ancient capital of the Byzantine Empire. The Ottoman Empire gave the city a new name, Istanbul, and changed the official religion from Christianity to Islam, turning cathedrals into mosques. Greece, Bulgaria, and most of Serbia now served the Ottoman sultan. The other Christian

Vlad III used impaling to intimidate his subjects and enemies.

Mohammed II conquered Constantinople in 1453.

nations of Europe, paralyzed by petty quarrels, were too weak and divided to prevent Mohammed from conquering Wallachia, Transylvania, and the rest of the Balkan peninsula.

But the valley of corpses left by Vlad III stopped Mohammed. "The sultan, overcome by amazement, admitted that he could not win the land from a man who does such things," wrote one historian, "and above all knows how to exploit his rule and that of his subjects in this way." Mohammed decided not to continue into Transylvania. Instead, he struck camp and turned back toward his palace in Istanbul. For now, he would not ask his men to fight this strange and terrifying monster. His own people had nicknamed Vlad Tepes: Vlad the Impaler.

A woodcut print of the historical Dracula

Chapter **TWO**

SON OF THE DRAGON

VLAD **III,** THE PRINCE OF WALLACHIA AND SWORN enemy of the Muslim Turks, had lived in violence and fear almost since the day he was born in 1431. Vlad's father, Vlad II or Vlad Dracul, and his mother, a Moldavian princess, lived in Transylvania, a region north of Wallachia that makes up the northwestern quarter of present-day Romania. The house where Vlad III was born, in the town of Sighisoara, still stands. Here Vlad Dracul's son, called Dracula, spent the first four years of his life with his parents and his brothers, Mircea and Radu.

At the time of his son's birth, Vlad Dracul was serving as the military governor of Transylvania. He ruled over cities populated by Hungarians, Romanians, and

German-speaking Saxons. Vlad Dracul's father had been a respected voivode (prince), and like many rulers, both spent most of their time plotting and fighting, mainly against the Ottoman Turks, against a rival clan of princes called the Danesti, and against the rebellious boyars (landowning nobles). Vlad II's greatest ambition was to defeat his Danesti rival and establish his family as the permanent hereditary rulers of Wallachia, his home country.

Transylvania and Wallachia were ruled by strength and treachery, not by law. The boyars held absolute power over their landless serfs, the peasants who worked the land in service of their masters. Rivalry between the boyars and the princes led to many civil wars, in which thousands of Transylvanians fought and died. And the borders of Transylvania were as chaotic and unstable as its government. To the southeast was the powerful Ottoman Empire. To the north was Hungary, whose rulers saw the weak Balkan principalities (countries ruled by princes) as lands ripe for conquest.

Hungary and the Ottoman Empire stood on the front lines of a much wider conflict between the Christian and Islamic religions. For about one hundred years, the Muslim Turks had been attacking and conquering Christian lands in Europe. The Ottoman sultans already controlled many parts of the Balkan peninsula, including Bulgaria, Wallachia, Greece, Bosnia, and Serbia. As the Turks advanced into new territory, they installed local princes to rule their conquests. Gradually, as their annual taxes were increased, these regions grew poorer and less able to defend themselves. Eventually, they were annexed as Ottoman provinces and ruled directly by the sultan.

The Christian leaders of central and western Europe faced the Turkish threat with powerful armies of their own. But the complicated rivalries between these leaders weakened their power. The largest Christian state of all, the Holy Roman Empire, was no more than a collection of dozens of small, independent kingdoms and principalities in central Europe. The Holy Roman Emperor exercised little control over these states.

In the early 1400s, the fight against the Turks still seemed too far away to pose a serious threat to the Holy Roman Empire. The pope, who was the leader of the Catholic church, could not convince Christian and Catholic rulers to coordinate an attack on the Turks. The ruler of the Byzantine Empire, a Christian state that was struggling to hold off the Turks in the Balkans and Asia Minor, was losing ground. In the middle of this conflict between Christianity and Islam stood Wallachia, Transylvania, and the three sons of Vlad Dracul.

VASSALS OF THE SULTAN

Because he controlled a frontier region, Vlad Dracul was called upon to help Christian Europe defend itself against Turkish attacks. In recognition of Vlad Dracul's service, Holy Roman Emperor Sigismund made him a member of the Order of the Dragon. This secret society was made up of knights who pledged loyalty to the emperor and vowed to protect Christian Europe against the Ottoman Empire. Vlad's membership in the Order of the Dragon earned him his nickname of "Dracul," which means "dragon" or "devil" in the Romanian language. This honor was bestowed on Vlad in 1431; the son born to him the same year was nicknamed Dracula, "Son of the Dragon."

To keep his power and to stay alive, a leader like Vlad Dracul had to conquer land and bring new subjects—mostly peasants—under his rule. With more land, he would be assured more income and soldiers; with less land, he would be weak, inviting attack from the outside. In his effort to gain more land and stay in power, Vlad Dracul formed alliances with Hungarians, Wallachians, and even Turks.

In 1437, Vlad Dracul brought an army out of Transylvania, invaded Wallachia, and murdered his Danesti rival, Alexandru. Vlad became the new prince of Wallachia. While Vlad was considered an ally and vassal (servant or subject) of Hungary, he still had to pay an annual tribute of money to the Ottoman sultan to protect himself from attack. In the next year, Vlad Dracul joined the Turks in their campaign against his former homeland, Transylvania, seeing this fight as the best way to consolidate his power in the region.

Nevertheless, the Ottoman sultan Murad II doubted Vlad's loyalty. In 1442, when Dracula was eleven years

Balkan Peninsula in Vlad Dracula's Day

Modern Balkan Peninsula

Danube R.
AUSTRIA
Budapest
ROMANIA
MOLDOVA
HUNGARY
SLOVENIA
Sighisoara
CARPATHIAN MTNS.
CROATIA
Sibiu
Brasov
BOSNIA AND HERZE-GOVINA
Bucarest
ITALY
SERBIA
Danube R.
BULGARIA
MONTENEGRO
BLACK SEA
ALBANIA
MACEDONIA
GREECE
Istanbul
TURKEY

Former Ottoman Empire

SICILY

CRETE

Prague
BOHEMIA

Danube River
BAVARIA
AUSTRIA
Munich
Salzburg
Vienna

HOLY ROMAN EMPIRE

Buda
H U N G A R Y
CARPATHIAN MTNS.
TRANSYLVANIA
MOLDAVIA
Sighisoara
Sibiu
Brasov
WALLACHIA
Olt R.
Arges R.
Tirgoviste

SLAVONIA

VENICE
CROATIA
Florence
PAPAL STATES
BOSNIA
SERBIA
Varna
BLACK SEA
Rome
A D R I A T I C   S E A
HERZEGOVINA
Kosovo
BULGARIA
Naples
ALBANIA
MACEDONIA
THRACE
OTTOMAN
Constantinople (Istanbul)
KINGDOM OF TWO SICILIES
EPIRUS
THESSALY
AEGEAN SEA
EMPIRE
Palermo
ATHENS
Egrigoz (Emet)
ANATOLIA (TURKEY)

CRETE

Legend

Ottoman Empire
Holy Roman Empire
Papal States

Miles
0   50   100   150

0   150
Kilometers

old, Murad tricked Vlad Dracul, as well as Dracula and his seven-year-old brother Radu, into riding south, across the Danube River into territory directly controlled by the Turks. Dracul and his sons were captured and brought to prison. To escape his imprisonment and return to Wallachia, Vlad Dracul pledged the lives of his sons against his own loyalty. The sultan allowed him to return to Wallachia, while Dracula and Radu remained behind as hostages.

Prisoner of the Turks

The sons of Vlad Dracul were brought to Egrigoz, a town in the region of Asia Minor, which lies between the Black Sea and the eastern Mediterranean Sea. The brothers remained imprisoned there for several years, suffering loneliness and torture. Meanwhile, their father forgot his pledge of loyalty to the sultan and joined a new fight against the Turks led by John Hunyadi, a Hungarian. In 1444, Hunyadi and his army were defeated by the Turks in the Battle of Varna, on the shores of the Black Sea. Hunyadi managed to escape from the Turkish army, but his cowardly flight from the battlefield angered Vlad Dracul. The prince helped seize Hunyadi and put him on trial.

Hunyadi eventually escaped both the Wallachians and the Turks. He swore revenge against Vlad Dracul and allied with Vladislav II, a member of the Danesti clan. With Vladislav's help, Hunyadi carried out his threat in 1447. Vlad Dracul was cruelly murdered along with his eldest son Mircea, whose eyes were put out with wooden stakes before he was buried alive.

In the meantime, Dracula and Radu had somehow survived their father's disloyalty to the sultan. The sultan may have believed that he could make Vlad Dracul's sons into obedient vassals. In 1448, the Turks released Dracula. The sultan sent him back to Europe with a plan to help him seize the throne of Wallachia from Vladislav II. Radu, Dracula's brother, stayed behind. Nicknamed "Radu the Handsome," he remained loyal to the Turks.

PRINCE OF WALLACHIA

When Dracula arrived in Wallachia, Vladislav II was away from his palace in Tirgoviste on a campaign with Hunyadi. Dracula easily captured the palace and proclaimed himself prince of Wallachia. He was cunning and brave, but only seventeen years old. And now that his father was dead, he found that he had few friends in Wallachia. His first reign as prince lasted only two months. Fearing assassination at the hands of the boyars or by Hunyadi's men, Dracula fled to Moldavia, where he took refuge for three years at the court of his cousin Stephen, the prince of Moldavia.

In his battles against the Turks, Hunyadi sought powerful allies wherever he could find them. In 1451, when Dracula fled a civil war in Moldavia, Hunyadi took him under his wing—even though Hunyadi had murdered Dracula's father! Hunyadi brought Dracula along on his campaigns in the Balkans and taught the younger man the arts of war and diplomacy. Dracula learned how to fight, how to command soldiers, and how to campaign against the Turkish armies.

The soldiers of Dracula's day fought with swords, knives, crossbows, and long spears known as pikes. Members of the Christian armies were recruited from among the peasants of Europe. These soldiers campaigned for several months or years and then returned to civilian life. The knights on horseback who fought in these campaigns were professional soldiers who took an oath of loyalty to a prince or king. The knights were well armed and well protected by armor and suits of chain mail. A skilled knight on horseback was the armored tank of medieval warfare, nearly unstoppable in battle.

The Ottoman armies used similar weapons, but they enjoyed an important advantage. The Turkish army included a large corps of professional soldiers known as janissaries. The janissaries spent their entire lives, from the time they were young boys, learning how to fight and survive on long campaigns. They were well equipped, since the sultan spent most of the taxes he collected on his military forces. As a result of their better training and equipment, the Turks were defeating even the largest armies that marched into the Balkans.

Fifteenth-century battle weapons were quite elaborate.

In 1453, the new Turkish sultan, Mohammed II, brought an army of as many as four hundred thousand soldiers to the gates of Constantinople. The Turks set up a land and naval blockade, bombarded the high city walls with cannon, and after several weeks captured the city. The Byzantine emperor, Constantine XI Dragases of the Dynasty Paleologus, was killed in the battle, and his empire immediately collapsed. The Turks prepared to swing north through the Balkans and, eventually, conquer all of Central Europe. They looked for help from loyal vassals, including Vladislav II of Wallachia, who had switched sides and was now fighting John Hunyadi's army.

Hunyadi asked Vlad Dracula to seize and defend Wallachia, the province that protected the mountain passes to Transylvania and the route to his homeland, Hungary. In 1456, Dracula captured and beheaded Vladislav II and once again took over the throne of Wallachia. This time, with a small army to protect him, he no longer feared that he would be assassinated by his political enemies. He only had to contend with the jealous Wallachian boyars, who in these chaotic times showed little respect for any man who would claim the title of prince.

Vlad Dracula had learned much from his days as a prisoner of the Turks. He had learned the Turkish language and many Turkish customs, including the torture of impalement. He took a special interest in this gruesome practice, in which a long wooden stake was pierced into a victim's body and then planted in the ground. Over several hours or days, the victim would slide down the stake under the force of his own weight, destroying the internal organs and causing the person to bleed to death.

Dracula was ready to use impalement or any other means he could think of to subdue his enemies and remain in power. At the same time, he was determined to win the respect and fear of the common people of Wallachia. In the first months of his reign, he staged a spectacle that would accomplish both goals.

Dracula invited the boyars to a council at his palace in Tirgoviste. In one of the many great halls, he held a sumptuous feast and a grand reception. There was music during the feast, as well as laughter, games, and conversation. During the festivities, Dracula asked the boyars their opinion of him and of the other princes who had come before him. Although he posed the question in a friendly manner, they answered rudely, as he knew they would. Dracula then ordered his servants to enter the room and seize the boyars. Ropes held the nobles while sharp stakes were driven through their bodies. The stakes were then set up in a field near the palace, where the boyars died in plain sight of the townspeople and peasants of the region.

The Impaler had taught his first lesson.

Dracula's notoriety grew as word of his cruel executions spread.

Chapter **THREE**

THE IMPALER

VOIVODE DRACULA WAS DETERMINED TO HOLD
onto power using the most effective weapon he knew:
terror. But Dracula was also shrewd and practical. His
first goal was to end the Saxons' control of trade in
Wallachia. The German-speaking Saxons bought and
sold goods between western Europe and the Balkan
peninsula. As traders, they competed directly with the
native Wallachian merchants, who did not have the
means to transport their own goods across Europe.
Dracula's campaign against the Saxon merchants led
to many terrible acts that would give him a bad name
through the centuries.

In the late 1450s, Dracula began a series of raids on
Saxon cities throughout Transylvania, including Sibiu

and Brasov. The prince ordered thousands of Saxon merchants and traders to be impaled and displayed outside the city walls to frighten the surviving inhabitants. At a place called Timpa Hill, near Brasov, Dracula once had his servants set up hundreds of impaled Saxon merchants in a large circle. He then sat down to a picnic among the dead and the dying.

A Bad Reputation

Dracula's subjects soon realized that no one was safe from the long wooden stakes or from the other methods of torture and death dreamed up by the prince. Some people were roasted over open fires; others were boiled alive. Dracula's servants and soldiers skinned, blinded, stabbed, drowned, maimed, and beheaded thousands of people. Men, women, children, and old people suffered; Saxons, Wallachians, Transylvanians, and Turks died. Victims served as examples or were punished for being part of a group that Dracula considered his enemy.

Dracula had no pity and rarely showed mercy. He did not tolerate crime, disloyalty, or dishonesty of any sort. Captured thieves and other criminals were promptly executed. According to one story, Dracula set a golden cup in a public square in the middle of Tirgoviste, daring anyone to steal it. The cup stood untouched throughout his reign.

According to another story, Dracula invited all the sick, disabled, and poor inhabitants of his land, as well as beggars and people suspected of petty crimes, to a party in a great hall in Tirgoviste. The sick and poor people were treated to a fabulous feast and celebration. As the party grew uproarious, the doors of the hall were bolted shut and the building was burned to the ground. No one survived the fire.

No place that Dracula's armies could reach was safe from burning, looting, and a bloody mass execution. Soon Dracula had achieved his goal—everyone who had seen or heard about these acts was terrified of him. But the most important source of Dracula's reputation for cruelty may have been his raids on the churches and monasteries belonging to the Roman Catholic Church—the church of the Saxons. Dracula's own religion was Eastern Orthodox, the eastern branch of Christianity. Dracula's attacks on the Catholics forced many people to flee the region. After reaching safety in central and western Europe, these refugees spread many tales—some of them true and some exaggerated—about the evil Wallachian prince.

DEFYING THE TURKS

Among the people of Wallachia, however, Dracula was also renowned for his heroism in battle. In Dracula's day, a leader's skill and cunning on the battlefield made up the most important part of his reputation. His subjects admired his success against the enemy, who was bringing fear to every corner of Christian Europe: the Ottoman Empire.

By the time of Dracula's second reign, the Turkish armies seemed invincible. They had overrun Greece, Bulgaria, and much of Serbia. In 1453, they had conquered Constantinople, the most important Christian city of eastern Europe. The Ottoman Empire threatened to spread north through the Balkan peninsula and overtake Hungary. The Turks might even attack Vienna; from this city they could advance on Germany or on Rome, the home of the Christian pope. Many Europeans feared they would soon become subjects of the Muslim sultan.

Nevertheless, the rulers of Christian Europe hesitated to unite their forces against the Turks. Military campaigns were very expensive and often risky, and the Christian countries had other battles to fight, including wars and intrigues against their rivals in the rest of Europe. In the Balkans, Christian rulers such as Vladislav II even joined with the Turks at times to strengthen their own armies. Vlad Dracul, Dracula's father, had himself switched sides in his many battles with the boyars and with his Danesti rivals.

Dracula, however, devoted much of his life to driving the Turks from Europe. In 1459, three years after the start of his second reign, Dracula defied the sultan by refusing to pay the expected annual tribute of money and soldiers. In 1461, the angry sultan sent two men—a Turk named Hamsa Pasha and a Greek named Catabolinos—to meet with Dracula and try to persuade him to make the tribute. The men had

Mohammed II fighting at Belgrade in the Balkan Peninsula

secret orders to trick Dracula into leaving his palace. At the first opportunity, they would put him in chains and bring him to Istanbul, the Ottoman capital.

But the sultan had not counted on Dracula's cunning. The prince got wind of the plan even before the two men reached his palace at Tirgoviste. When Hamsa Pasha and Catabolinos arrived, they were captured and impaled along with several hundred other enemies of the prince. Dracula ordered that Hamsa Pasha be given the highest stake in honor of his rank. From this point on, Dracula and the Turkish sultan were sworn enemies.

DRACULA'S CRUSADE

In the meantime, the pope had called on the leaders of Europe to unite against the Turks. Although many of these rulers promised to join the crusade, in the end few did so. Dracula was an important exception. In 1461, he gathered an army and marched across the Danube River, which separated Wallachia from the Ottoman-ruled territory of Bulgaria. His soldiers captured and destroyed many Turkish forts and cities along the river. Cities and fields were burned and thousands of people died in battle or were executed. But when Dracula finally reached the Black Sea, he found that he had been trapped and outnumbered. Mohammed had mounted a counterattack.

As Dracula retreated, Turkish and Bulgarian soldiers marched north toward Wallachia, making their way to Dracula's capital at Tirgoviste. The sultan crossed the Danube River in June 1462, while Dracula turned and led his army westward through Wallachia. Much in need of reinforcements, Dracula sent urgent messages to Matthias Corvinus, the new king of Hungary, asking for help. Matthias promised to come to Dracula's aid. He assembled an army at his capital of Buda and began marching south toward Transylvania and the Carpathian Mountains.

As Dracula's army retreated toward Transylvania, the soldiers destroyed farms, burned fields, and emptied cities of all their food and wares. They dumped the carcasses of dead livestock into wells to poison the water. Guerrilla fighters ambushed Turks who were searching for food in the Wallachian forests. Dracula also sent people who were infected with diseases to mingle with the Turks. Soon members of the Turkish army at Tirgoviste were dying of the plague and other illnesses. Around this time, Dracula also ordered the terrifying mass impalement that daunted Mohammed and the Turkish army.

Unable to catch the Wallachian army, and unnerved by Dracula's cruelty, the sultan abandoned the campaign and returned to his capital. Instead of following Dracula into the Carpathian Mountains, Mohammed left a large part of his army in Tirgoviste under the leadership of Dracula's brother, Radu the Handsome, who had accompanied the sultan. Mohammed promised to help Radu claim and hold the throne of Wallachia. In Tirgoviste, Radu commanded soldiers from the Turkish army as well as private armies of the boyars who sought Dracula's destruction.

THE PRISONER

In the fall of 1462, while still retreating, Dracula took shelter in a castle on the Arges River. The castle, which Dracula had built early in his reign, stood high on a cliff overlooking the river. The thick walls and high towers allowed a small group to hold out for a long time against a much larger enemy force. Castle Dracula was designed to protect the prince from his many enemies—the boyars, the Saxons, and rival princes in Transylvania and Hungary. For a brief time, it sheltered Dracula from the army chasing him into the mountains.

The Turks surrounded the castle and prepared to storm it. Outnumbered and cornered, Dracula decided to escape through a secret passage that led from the castle down to a cave along the river. At night, with a small group of soldiers, he fled the castle and made his way north, away from the Turkish army. Dracula's company followed narrow trails and steep footpaths along high mountain passes until they finally reached

These are the ruins of Vlad Dracula's castle at Poenari Hill.

the city of Brasov. Here Matthias Corvinus and his army of Hungarians were waiting for Dracula.

Although Matthias had promised to help, Dracula did not trust him. Dracula knew that the Hungarian king wanted to control Transylvania and Wallachia and that Dracula's own powerful army and prestige as a crusader against the Turks stood in the way. Dracula and Matthias spent several weeks negotiating their future alliance. Meanwhile, Radu the Handsome, Dracula's brother, ruled Wallachia with the support of the Turks as well as the boyars, who feared nothing as much as the return of the Impaler.

Matthias finally agreed to place soldiers at Dracula's disposal. Dracula would use these men to attack Tirgoviste. Matthias would then arrive with a much larger force. Dracula and Jan Jiskra, the leader of Matthias's army, returned to the Carpathians, where they made their headquarters at a fortress known as Konigstein. A few days later, when the company began climbing down a steep valley, Jiskra's men suddenly seized Dracula. They brought him back to Brasov, where Matthias Corvinus made him a prisoner. In December 1462, Dracula was marched several hundred miles north, away from Wallachia, to the Hungarian capital of Buda. He had been tricked.

THE DEATH OF DRACULA

Matthias needed to justify Dracula's imprisonment to the other leaders of Europe—many of whom still

This grave at the Snagov Monastery in Romania is said to hold the bones of Dracula.

admired Dracula for his success in fighting their enemy, the Turks. So Matthias accused him of betraying the Christians of Europe. As evidence, several letters were brought forth showing that Dracula had written to the Turkish sultan. In the letters, Dracula offered to stop making war on the Turks and to help the sultan in his campaigns against Transylvania. Many historians believe that these letters were fakes.

Dracula was forced to spend the next several years in Hungary. He lived in the fortress of Visegrad, on the Danube River near Buda. Although he was not locked up like other prisoners, he could not return to his homeland, which was now under the control of his brother Radu.

King Matthias offered to free Dracula if he would abandon the Orthodox Church and become a Roman

Catholic. (Hungary was a Catholic land, while the people of Wallachia belonged to the Eastern Orthodox church). If Dracula would convert, Matthias would support him once again as the prince of Wallachia. If he did not convert, he would stay at the fortress of Visegrad.

Dracula wanted above all to return to Wallachia. He accepted the offer to convert to Catholicism. Meanwhile, Radu had lost the throne of Wallachia to Basarab the Old, who was supported by Dracula's cousin, Stephen of Moldavia. Soon afterward, Radu died. In 1475, Dracula moved to Sibiu, Transylvania.

The following year, Dracula invaded Wallachia with the help of Prince Stephen Bathory of Transylvania. When Basarab the Old learned that the Impaler was back, he fled with his supporters. Dracula took the throne for the third time in his life. But this time, his reign was very brief. The boyars quickly gathered their forces, and the many enemies Dracula had made over the years proved too powerful for him. Another Turkish army invaded, and near the city of Bucharest, Dracula was separated from his own army, surrounded, and killed—perhaps by Turkish soldiers, perhaps by the Wallachian boyars. His head was cut off and sent to the Turkish capital at Istanbul, where it was displayed for all to see. According to legend, Dracula's headless corpse was buried at the monastery of Snagov, not far from Bucharest, the modern capital of Romania.

THE LEGEND OF PRINCE DRACULA

Dracula's death put an end to his tortures, murders, and gruesome impalements. But he was not forgotten in Wallachia and Transylvania. People in the region had seen many cruel rulers, but Prince Dracula stood above them all for his sheer ferocity as well as his great ability as a soldier. Tales and legends about him began to spread. People told about the time Dracula had impaled a woman because she had not properly mended her husband's shirt. Once, another story went, two Turks came to Dracula's court without removing the turbans from their heads, and Dracula ordered that the hats be nailed to their skulls. A boyar had once complained of the smell coming from Dracula's impaled victims—Dracula ordered this boyar to be impaled on a stake much taller than the others, so that he would not have to suffer from the stench.

In Germany, people also told Dracula stories. To them, Dracula was no hero for fighting against the Turks. Instead, he was a monster and a tyrant. Using the printing press, a new invention, German writers created small illustrated books called pamphlets to sell to the public. Some of these pamphlets told sensational stories about Dracula, written by German monks who had fled from Transylvania. The cover of one pamphlet, printed in Nuremberg, Germany, in 1499, shows Dracula picknicking among the bodies of his impaled victims near Brasov. The picture's caption reads: "Here begins a very cruel, frightening story

Graphic illustrations often appeared in pamphlets that told of the horrors of Vlad Dracula.

Die facht fich an gar ein grauffem
liche erfch:ockenliche hyftorien von dem wilden wütrich.
Dracole wayde. Wie er die leüt gefpist hat. vnd gepraten,
vnd mit den haüstern yn einem keffel gefoten. vñ wie er die
leüt gefchunden hat vñ zerhacken laffen als ein kraut. Jtes
er hat auch den mütern ire kind gepraté vnd fy habes müf/
fen felber effen. Vnd vil andere erfchrockenliche ding die in
diffem Tractat gefchriben ftend. Vnd in welchem land er
geregiret hat.

about a wild bloodthirsty man, Dracula the voevod. How he impaled people and roasted them . . . and how he skinned people and hacked them into pieces like the head of a cabbage . . . "

Over the centuries, millions of people in Europe read and heard tales about the legendary Prince Dracula. But nobody took him for anything more than a very human murderer. He did not become a blood-sucking, undead vampire until the imagination of Irish writer Bram Stoker turned him into one.

PART II

BRAM STOKER'S DRACULA

Chapter **FOUR**

VAMPIRES

EUROPE HAS CHANGED IN THE FIVE HUNDRED YEARS since Vlad Dracula reigned in Wallachia. Jets and fast trains carry travelers from one city and country to the next. Trucks, cars, and motor scooters crowd the roads and freeways. Telephones and computers allow people to communicate instantly. All over the world, scientists and doctors have solved many of the problems posed by disease and poverty. Superstitions have become stories to tell in movies and books. Still, one mystery remains: what happens to us after we die.

Ever since human beings realized death would come to them, they have tried to solve this mystery. Myths and stories were written that attempted to answer the puzzle of death. Religions promised believers a heaven for the faithful and a hell for sinners after death. Angels, spirits, and ghosts, who came from the world of the dead, appeared in religious texts as well as stories and legends. One of these legendary creatures is said to have survived death to walk among the living and feed on their blood. This undead being was called *wampir* in the languages of Serbia and Hungary. From this eastern European word came the English word *vampire*.

Different societies all over the world have believed in vampires. In ancient Greece, mothers reminded naughty children about the dreadful lamia, the evil spirit of a mythical queen from Africa. The lamia had a human head and a serpent's tail. In a jealous rage against Zeus, the king of the gods, Queen Lamia kidnapped and killed all the children she could find. With sweet music she lured sailors to her distant lair, then drank their blood and ate their flesh.

Vampire lore survives in modern Greece, where the word for vampire is *vrukalakos*. Many regions of Greece as well as the Balkans are still said to be haunted by the undead. The Greek island of Santorini, which lies along the rim of a dormant volcano, has a reputation as the home of vampires.

The people of ancient Assyria, Babylon, Egypt, and Rome also spread vampire tales. Vampire legends exist in India, China, South America, Haiti, and Africa. In many of these places the vampire is a horrifying animal.

VAMPIRE SUPERSTITIONS

In the Middle Ages (A.D. 500 to 1500), the vampire myths of ancient Greece and Rome spread northward to the rest of Europe, where vampires took on human form. Vampirism became a fearful superstition as an answer to the riddle of life after death.

In those years, people were sometimes accidentally buried alive. During times of disease or plague, sick or dying people might be disposed of too quickly for fear they would infect others. But some who were thought to be dead were only in a trance or a state of shock. From time to time, when coffins were dug up and opened, there were signs that the corpse had struggled after burial. Blood was found in the coffin and on the burial shroud. Vampirism was suspected.

In medieval Europe, people believed there were many different ways to become a vampire. For example, a person who committed suicide might turn into a vampire. Since churches would not bury suicide victims in holy ground, people feared restless spirits might return to haunt their families. For good measure, wooden stakes were driven through the bodies of suicides to keep them from wandering at night.

Children who died without being baptized were also thought to become vampires. So were criminals and witches. In the Balkans and the Mediterranean region, anyone with uncommon features, such as red hair or blue eyes, was suspected of vampirism. Birth defects and mental illness were also cause for superstition. A

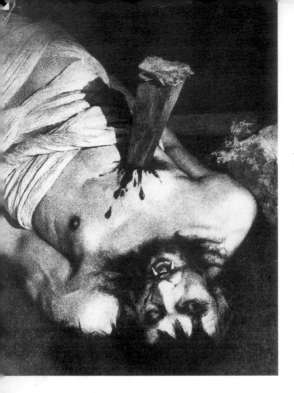

A stake through the heart was thought to keep a vampire dead.

cat leaping over a dead body or a bird flying overhead during a burial was thought to bring on vampirism.

According to legend, vampires could change themselves into other forms, such as a bat or a wolf or even a cloud of mist that could pass under doors and through keyholes. It was said that vampires walked at night and returned to their graves during the day. They favored misty swamps, dark caves, abandoned mines, cemeteries, or anywhere normal, living people feared to go. Vampires were thought to have long fingernails, staring eyes, and terrible bad breath.

Vampires allegedly preyed on their families and relatives, and their bite caused a wasting sickness that eventually killed their victims. Those believed to have suffered a vampire attack were thought to become vampires after death.

Believers could use several weapons to protect themselves against vampires. Garlic flowers and bulbs were hung up in a doorway or anyplace a vampire could get in to a home: a chimney flue, a window, a keyhole. People wore crucifixes or displayed them on their doors or walls, believing that vampires could not stand the sight of the cross. They also believed that vampires could not cross running water, nor could they enter a circle made with holy water.

Legends tell of certain ways to find a vampire. Suspected corpses were dug up and carefully examined. Normally, a dead person's hair and fingernails continue to grow while the skin and organs decompose. But if the body wasn't rotting normally, the person was thought to be a vampire. If a vampire was found, it had to be destroyed by driving a stake through its heart while it rested in its grave. The head had to be cut off and thrown onto a bonfire. These methods were thought to keep the vampire in its resting place—permanently.

THE VAMPIRE OF MEDEUGNA

Belief in vampires was strongest in Central Europe and the Balkans, where Vlad Dracula had lived and died. Serbia, Transylvania, Poland, Slovakia, and Wallachia all experienced deadly waves of vampire panics. Crop failures, disease epidemics, droughts, livestock deaths, even unexplained disappearances were often blamed on vampires. During these panics, a sort of hysteria or fear, based on superstition, rumor, and gossip overcame the population. Many innocent people suspected of being vampires were executed, just as many suspected witches in North America were once subject to trial and death. One of the worst vampire panics in history took place in the Balkans in the early 1730s.

During this time, a young Serbian man named Arnold Poele came home from his army service in Greece and the Middle East. Poele settled near a village called Medeugna, near Belgrade in Serbia (then under Ottoman control). He bought a house and some land, raised crops, and for several years lived a normal life.

Poele was not entirely normal, however. He told many strange tales of his time in Greece. Once, he claimed, he had been visited by the spirit of a dead man. To rid himself of this spirit, he had opened the grave and driven a stake through the corpse. Later Poele had left Greece and the army and had returned to Serbia.

During one fall harvest, Poele slipped and fell from a tall hay wagon. Soon after the accident, he died. The villagers gave him a Christian funeral and laid him to rest in the church cemetery. But they had not seen the last of Arnold Poele. Not long after the funeral, many people reported that they had seen Poele walking about the village at night. After these visions, the witnesses fell ill. They grew extremely weak, as if from a heavy loss of blood. Several of them died, and the villagers grew so afraid of Poele that they stopped going out of their houses at night.

The leaders of Medeugna decided to put Poele's spirit to rest. They marched to the church graveyard, bringing along several army officers and surgeons. The vampire historian Montague Summers described the scene:

> Before very long the coffin was rather roughly dragged out of the ground, and the gravedigger's assistant soon knocked off the lid. It was seen that the corpse had moved to one side, the jaws gaped wide open, and the blue lips were moist with new blood which had trickled in a thin stream from the corner of the mouth. All un-afraid, the old sexton caught the body and twisted it straight. "So," he cried, "you have not wiped your mouth since last night's work."

Instead of rotting and stinking, Arnold Poele's corpse had remained quite healthy looking: a sure sign of vampirism. The officers threw garlic down on Poele's corpse and then drove a stake through its chest. Poele's victims were also dug up and staked through the heart. The bodies of Arnold Poele and four other villagers were then thrown on a great bonfire. From that time on, the village slept peacefully.

A STORMY NIGHT, A VAMPIRE TALE

Even in Poele's time, most doctors and scientists didn't pay attention to superstitions like vampire stories. After all, the eighteenth century was known as the Age of Reason. Europe's philosophers believed that every mystery could be explained in a reasonable way. Science was beginning to answer the questions people asked about life and nature. Education became more widely available. As people learned to read and write, reliance upon legends and tales began to fade.

Nevertheless, real cases of vampirism occur from time to time. Doctors call it hematomania—the desire to drink blood. In the 1940s, an Englishman named John Haigh was arrested for murdering several people and then drinking their blood. Centuries earlier, a seventeenth-century Hungarian Countess named Elizabeth Bathory bathed in the blood of her victims, young girls whom she hired as servants and then tortured and murdered. For her crimes, Bathory was put on trial and sentenced to be walled up in a room of her castle.

The Age of Reason made superstitions and irrational fears into curiosities—and material for fiction. In the late 1700s, European writers began creating a new kind of story called the Gothic novel. These books were filled with ghosts, spirits, and lots of mysterious events. Gothic novels were set in ruined castles or in haunted or isolated places in the mountains or along the sea-coast. The action took place during dark and stormy nights, when wise men and women stayed indoors and spirits walked the earth.

One stormy night during the summer of 1816, a group of English friends were staying at a villa on the shores of Lake Geneva in Switzerland. The weather had been rainy for many days, so they passed the time by reading horror stories. That night, a poet named Lord Byron challenged the rest of the group to write their own ghost stories. The guests set to work. An eighteen-year-old woman, Mary Wollstonecraft Shelley, started *Frankenstein,* a story about a scientist who sets out to create an ideal human being in his laboratory. Byron himself started a vampire tale but never finished it. John Polidori, Byron's doctor, wrote a tale called *The Vampyre,* which became the first vampire

Lady Bathory committed her crimes in this castle.

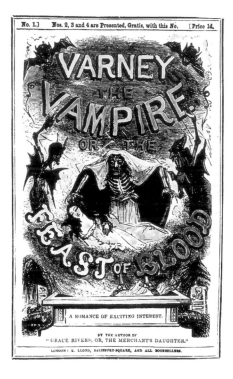

Vampire stories like this one were popular in England.

story ever published in the English language.

After Polidori's story appeared, vampires caught on fast with authors in England, France, and Germany. *Varney the Vampire or the Feast of Blood,* written by James Malcolm Rymer, appeared in 1847, published in several installments in an English magazine. Rymer filled the 220 chapters of his story with hundreds of frightening, supernatural scenes.

Horror tales became standard fare for publishers of books and magazines. In fact, some of the best novels of the nineteenth century described supernatural events. Oscar Wilde wrote *The Picture of Dorian Gray,* in which a painted portrait mysteriously changes. Robert Louis Stevenson wrote *The Strange Case of Dr. Jekyll and Mr. Hyde.* The detective Sherlock Holmes solves the mystery of the walking undead in *The Sussex Vampire,* by Sir Arthur Conan Doyle. One of the best-known vampire tales was *Carmilla,* by the Irish writer Joseph Sheridan Le Fanu. At the end of *Carmilla,* a vampire is destroyed by having a stake driven through its heart and its head cut off. The stake through the heart became one of the most popular conventions of vampire stories that followed.

Sometime in the early 1870s, a young Irish theater critic named Bram Stoker read *Carmilla.* Stoker was soon writing Gothic tales of his own. In 1881, he published a book of short horror stories called *Under the Sunset.* In 1890 he began work on a new book with a subject worthy of a full-length novel. His novel would describe the historical Vlad Tepes as Count Dracula, a 500-year-old vampire who brings terror and death to modern England.

Even as an adult, Bram Stoker liked to dream.

Chapter **FIVE**

BRAM STOKER

BRAM STOKER WAS BORN IN CLONTARF, IRELAND, in 1847. (His given name was Abraham, the same as his father. But the younger Stoker always called himself "Bram" for short.) For the first several years of his life, Bram suffered from a mysterious disease that prevented him from physical activity. He couldn't walk until he was seven years old, and for long periods of time he couldn't even get out of bed. He often spent his days reading or daydreaming. In the evening, he listened to his mother, Charlotte, tell Irish ghost stories. At the age of seven, Bram suddenly recovered from his illness and began taking part in games and sports with his friends. He grew tall and strong and became a good athlete.

Stoker's father worked in Dublin Castle, an imposing old fortress in the Irish capital city of Dublin. From this building, the government of the English queen ruled Ireland, setting down laws and keeping regulations and records. Abraham Stoker and hundreds of other clerks like him worked hard but earned little money. Although the job often frustrated the elder Stoker, he wanted his son to follow in his footsteps. He knew that in the civil service, Bram would have a steady income and a respectable job.

Bram Stoker was an obedient son, but he took more interest in the theater than in a civil-service career. He loved reading poetry and plays, delighting in the power of words to thrill and fascinate a reader. He read the plays of Shakespeare and the novels of Jonathan Swift, the author of *Gulliver's Travels*. Bram loved the Gothic-style novels of terror and romance, which reminded him of the stories that his mother had once recited at his bedside.

Bram Stoker was known to his friends as outgoing, reliable, and loyal. While attending Trinity College in Dublin, he joined debating societies, auditioned for plays, and won trophies in several different sports. After leaving Trinity, he dutifully followed his father's wishes and took a job in the civil service. He also started work on a thesis in mathematics. If he could finish the thesis, he would earn a master's degree and, possibly, find a better career as a university professor.

Stoker did not forget his fascination with writers

and the theater, however. He followed the careers of famous actors and took every opportunity he had to attend plays. In 1867, at the Theatre Royal in Dublin, Stoker saw the actor Henry Irving perform in a play called *The Rivals*. Irving's performance deeply impressed Stoker. Here was an actor with a very rare talent: the ability to make audiences feel the emotions of a character. After that night, Henry Irving had one more devoted fan. Stoker never missed a chance to see his idol perform.

Henry Irving portrays Shylock in William Shakespeare's The Merchant of Venice

WRITER AND MANAGER

In 1871, Stoker, began writing drama reviews for Dublin newspapers. These reviews earned him no pay and not even a credit line naming him as the author. But they did allow him to see as many plays as he liked and to follow the work of theatrical companies from Dublin and from London, considered at the time to be the center of the theater world. At the same time, Stoker began submitting his short stories to illustrated magazines. He sold his first story, "The Crystal Cup," to *London Society* in 1872.

In 1876, Henry Irving was playing in Dublin and read Stoker's complimentary reviews of his performance. Wanting to meet this enthusiastic critic, Irving invited Stoker to dinner. The two men quickly struck up a close friendship. Stoker could enjoy the excitement of the theater as an insider, and he gave Irving the attention and praise the actor craved. In 1878, when Irving began searching for a business manager for his own Lyceum Theatre, he turned to his devoted friend Bram Stoker.

The chance to travel and work with Henry Irving thrilled Stoker. He immediately quit his post at Dublin Castle and gave up all thoughts of a career as a professor. He had just married Florence Balcombe, a neighbor from Dublin; the couple would start their new life in an entirely new world. Stoker rushed to England to join Irving's theater company, which performed at the Lyceum in London and toured all over

Great Britain. From that point on, Bram Stoker's life revolved around Henry Irving.

As the theater's business manager, Stoker sold tickets, counted money, arranged travel, and took care of the theater's props, tools, and costumes. He worked long nights helping Irving and the other Lyceum actors during performances; he spent his days organizing the company's tours in Great Britain, Europe, and North America. He oversaw expensive dinners that Irving held for his friends in the Beefsteak Room, a fancy dining hall behind the Lyceum stage. Stoker also spent much of his time writing letters—thousands of them—to Irving's business associates, other actors, theater critics, and the actor's many fans.

Although Stoker's duties kept him very busy, he also found time to write short stories and novels. In 1890 he published his first novel, called *The Snake's Pass*. That same year, he came up with the idea that would turn into the novel *Dracula*. Inspired by popular tales of vampires and ghosts, Stoker created his own Gothic monster: a vampire who lives somewhere in a remote corner of Europe and crosses the sea to haunt the innocent people of England.

LEARNING ABOUT DRACULA

Stoker spent his nights at the Lyceum and worked by day to research his book. He learned as much as he could about central Europe and vampire superstitions. He carefully plotted the book by filling out a detailed schedule of dates and events. Stoker also learned about his subject from an expert named Arminius Vambéry.

This distinguished Hungarian professor had traveled all over the world and knew dozens of languages and their dialects. Disguised as a Muslim pilgrim, he had wandered through the Middle East and Central Asia, visiting shahs and emirs and speaking with them in their native languages. By the time he decided to visit London, his daring adventures had already made him quite a celebrity.

On April 30, 1890, Bram Stoker met Vambéry at a dinner in the Beefsteak Room. Just weeks earlier, Stoker had begun taking notes for his vampire novel. At the dinner, Vambéry told Stoker about his travels as well as the many legends about the sultan's court in Istanbul. He described the hills and forests of Transylvania and the tangled history of the Ottoman Empire's conquests in southeastern Europe. Vambéry also may have been the first person to tell Bram Stoker about Vlad the Impaler, the bloody prince of medieval Wallachia.

After meeting Vambéry, Stoker began spending hours in the Round Reading Room of the British Museum, studying travel and history books. He may have read some of the museum's fifteenth-century German pamphlets that described Prince Dracula. Another important source for Stoker's novel was *The Land Beyond the Forest*, a travel book about Transylvania. The author, an

Englishwoman named Emily Gerard, described the vampire superstitions of the peasants in Transylvania.

> More decidedly evil is the *nosferatu*, or vampire in which every Roumanian peasant believes as firmly as he does in heaven or hell. . . . every person killed by a nosferatu becomes likewise a vampire after death, and will continue to suck the blood of other innocent persons till the spirit has been exorcised by opening the grave of the suspected person, and either driving a stake through the corpse, or else firing a pistol-shot into the coffin.

Stoker, seated fourth from right, *and Irving,* standing fourth from left, *raised money for the Lyceum by hosting luncheons.*

The ruins of the real Whitby Abbey in North Yorkshire

In the summer of 1890, Stoker spent a vacation in Whitby, England, a small port on the North Sea coast. The town was split by a small river, the Esk, and its houses and shops rose along the sides of two steep hills. On top of a nearby cliff stood the ruins of the ancient Whitby Abbey, built long before the time of Prince Dracula himself.

Stoker walked through the town and climbed the steep stairs that led up the two hillsides. He strolled along the beach and the cliffs, imagining the terror of a vampire loose among the town's innocent inhabitants. He came up with a name for his main character: Count Wampyr. He studied books in the Whitby library, carefully jotting down facts to use in his novel. He borrowed *An Account of the Principalities of Wallachia and Moldavia,* by the historian William Wilkinson. In this book, Stoker read about Voivode Dracula and Wilkinson's explanation that Dracula in Romanian means "devil." Stoker changed the name of Count Wampyr to Count Dracula and continued working out the plot of his story, a story that took him seven years to finish. It was the story of a strange and frightening old count who lived in a dark, eerie, crumbling castle—alone.

Turn the page and read the story—if you dare. . . .

"But my very feelings changed to repulsion and terror when I
saw the whole man . . . crawl down the castle wall."

Chapter **SIX**

Bram Stoker's
Dracula

A YOUNG CLERK NAMED JONATHAN HARKER travels from England to the continent of Europe. Trains carry him through the great cities of Munich, Vienna, and Budapest, where he visits many wonderful and historic sights. But Harker is at work, not on vacation. He must travel further, to Transylvania, a mysterious region deep within the Balkan peninsula and far from the comfortable homes and friendly, bustling streets of England. In Transylvania he will meet a count who wishes to buy an old, ruined abbey in England.

Harker reaches the Borgo Pass, high in the Carpathian Mountains. The people here seem frightened, and Harker soon learns why. It is St. George's

Eve, the night when the spirits of the dead walk among the living. When the villagers learn that Harker is traveling to Castle Dracula, they shudder with fright and urge him not to go. Harker insists that he must continue. Business is business!

That night, Harker reaches the entrance of Castle Dracula. It is a strange, gloomy old fortress perched high on a steep cliff. The walls are tumbling down; the windows are dark and silent. The castle seems to be deserted. The Count himself opens the heavy wooden door for his guest. "Welcome to my house," he says. "Come freely. Go safely; and leave something of the happiness you bring!"

The Count leads Harker to the guest chambers. The rooms seem comfortable and cheerful enough, and a meal has been prepared. The Count offers Harker a cigar; a roaring fire warms the room. The two men begin talking about England. The Count seems very curious about the country he is soon to visit. He apologizes to Harker for his poor command of the English language, but Harker compliments the Count on his efforts. Indeed, Dracula seems like an intelligent man. But Harker can't help noticing the Count's strange, pale face, his long ears, his very sharp teeth, and his extremely bad breath.

Before he leaves his guest, Dracula offers a friendly warning. Harker is free to wander around the castle, as long as he doesn't try to enter the rooms that are locked. "Our ways are not your ways, and there shall be to you many strange things," Dracula explains. As dawn approaches, the Count leaves Harker, explaining that he must be away the next day.

Harker soon learns that the ways of Castle Dracula are stranger than he had imagined. There are no servants—Dracula lives alone in this frightening place. Worse, all the doors in the castle, including the front door, are locked. He is a prisoner! One night, Harker sneaks into a room next to his own. Three ghostly women approach him; he pretends to sleep. One seems about to bite him on the neck. Suddenly, the Count appears and drives them away, saying "This man belongs to me!"

Later, wondering what Dracula meant by those words, and how he will ever escape from the castle, Harker gazes out one of the high windows. Below is a fantastic gorge, thousands of feet deep. In the distance are the snow capped Carpathian Mountains. Just beneath him, he sees something much less scenic: the figure of the Count leaning out from another window. Dracula slowly emerges from the window and then crawls face-down, like a bat, along the castle wall.

The strange events begin to terrify Harker. It seems that Count Dracula has decided to make him a permanent guest. Instead of allowing Harker to leave, the Count asks Harker to write three letters home and date them in advance, so his friends will believe he is safe and sound. Meanwhile, Dracula prepares for the journey to his new home at Carfax Abbey in England.

"No trace has ever been found of the great dog."

He hires a band of gypsies to build wooden boxes. But instead of luggage or clothing, the boxes hold damp black earth from the crypt beneath the castle.

HAUNTING WHITBY

Meanwhile, in England, Harker's fiancée, Mina Murray, is worried. Jonathan has lost touch, which is not like him. When his letters finally arrive, his words sound distant and unfamiliar. As the weeks stretch on, Mina still has no sign that Jonathan will return.

Mina's friend Lucy Westenra seems to have all the luck: she gets three marriage proposals in one day!

But Lucy and Mina have been friends for a long time, and they won't let jealousy ruin their happy memories. They are spending the summer at a quaint old seaside fishing village called Whitby. The town rises on two sides of a steep valley, with a little stream running through the middle. On one side of the valley is a pretty old church, with a scary graveyard that stands right on the edge of the cliff. Lucy and Mina walk up the 199 steps to the church to enjoy the fine view and to talk with the interesting old fishermen who gather on the graveyard's stone benches.

From the churchyard, Mina and Lucy can see fishing boats trawl through the rough waters of the North Sea. The ocean looks dangerous, but the boat captains know its reefs and rocks. They can skillfully steer their boats through the tumbling waves into Whitby harbor.

One night, however, a Russian cargo boat has an unlucky accident. A terrible storm comes up, and the wrecked boat struggles into the harbor. When the police climb aboard the boat to investigate, they find that every single member of the crew has died. The yardarms are split; the torn sails flap wildly in the whistling gale. The dead captain is lashed to the wheel. The only survivor, a huge, fierce-looking dog, leapt from the boat as it crashed against the Whitby pier. Below deck is a strange cargo—nothing but boxes of earth, shipped to England from the castle of Count Dracula.

A Mysterious Illness

The death boat seems like a bad omen. Mina fears for Jonathan, but she can do nothing to bring him back to England. Not only is Jonathan far away from her, but Mina's friend Lucy has begun to act strangely. Lucy walks in her sleep and often wanders outside in her nightgown. One night, Mina sees Lucy sitting up on their favorite graveyard seat. Some kind of man or animal is bending over her, but in the dark Mina can't see very well. As she rushes up to the graveyard, the figure vanishes like a mist. Mina can see nobody there but her friend.

After that night, Lucy becomes mysteriously ill. She turns pale and weak and begins to suffer terrible nightmares. She continues to sleepwalk through Whitby. One of the men who proposed to her, Dr. Jonathan Seward, examines her but can find nothing wrong. Seward is a practical man of science who runs a lunatic asylum. To find the answer that must explain this mystery, he asks his friend and former teacher, Dr. Abraham Van Helsing, to rush to England from his home in Amsterdam. Van Helsing has treated many unusual diseases, and he will know what to do.

Van Helsing arrives and examines Lucy thoroughly. He begins to suspect what is wrong with her, but he won't tell anyone yet—not even Dr. Seward. One of the symptoms, however, frightens him: Lucy has lost a lot of blood. If the blood isn't replaced, she will die. Van Helsing immediately orders transfusions. Dr. Seward and Arthur Holmwood, Lucy's new fiancé, allow Van Helsing to draw their own blood and transfer it to Lucy's body. One of their friends, an American named Quincey Morris, also gives blood, as does Van Helsing himself. At night, Van Helsing orders the doors and windows of Lucy's room to be shut tight. He also hangs bulbs and flowers of garlic around the room. But the transfusions and the garlic don't seem to help. One night, Lucy's mother carelessly opens a window to let in some fresh air. Soon afterward, Lucy dies. The funeral takes place in London.

In the meantime, Jonathan Harker has returned from Transylvania. He has been gone for four months. He is weak and nearly in shock; clearly he has been through a terrible ordeal. But he's alive and breathing and back home in England. He begins a slow recovery that lasts until he sees a familiar, black-clad figure walking the streets of London. "It is the man himself!" he exclaims in despair.

STRANGE EVENTS

Soon after Harker spots Count Dracula, the London newspapers describe a series of strange events. A wolf disappears from a zoo, then reappears. Children are also vanishing. When they finally return, they babble nonsense about a beautiful lady who kidnaps them in the middle of the night.

By now, Van Helsing knows what he must do. First he must convince the others that Lucy has become a member of the undead—a vampire. One night, he brings Dr. Seward to the cemetery where the corpse of Lucy Westenra should be resting. The two men pry the lid off the coffin and find—nothing! The body has disappeared.

Later, the two men return to the cemetery in the daytime. This time, Lucy's corpse lies in its coffin, strangely fresh and well preserved. Dr. Seward is confused. Van Helsing then brings Arthur Holmwood and Seward to the graveyard at night. To their horror, they see Lucy walking among the yew trees and headstones, carrying a child in her arms. Holmwood stares at his undead fiancée. Her lips are crimson with fresh blood and she has a hungry, evil look in her eyes. "Come to me, Arthur," says the living corpse after tossing the baby to the ground. "Leave these others and come to me. My arms are hungry for you. Come, and we can rest together. Come, my husband, come!"

Seward and Holmwood are terrified. Van Helsing has been proven right. The men return during the day and open Lucy's coffin. Van Helsing gives Holmwood the weapons he will need: a heavy hammer and a sharpened wooden stake. While Van Helsing reads aloud a prayer for the dead, Holmwood drives the stake through Lucy's heart. "The Thing in the coffin writhed; and a hideous, blood-curdling screech came from the opened red lips. The body shook and quivered and twisted in wild contortions; the sharp white teeth champed together till the lips were cut, and the

mouth was smeared with a crimson foam." Soon the
struggle is finished. Lucy's face grows peaceful.

The group still must deal with Count Dracula, who
stalks London and who will soon be leading an army
of English vampires if he is not stopped. A few days
later, Van Helsing meets with the friends who have

*"My own heart grew cold as ice . . . as we recognized the
features of Lucy Westenra."*

gathered to fight the vampire. At the meeting Van Helsing explains that Dracula "must indeed have been that Voivode Dracula who won his name against the Turk." The creature they are fighting is none other than Vlad Tepes, the Impaler, the Prince Dracula of ancient Wallachia and Transylvania. He has returned to haunt the earth five hundred years after he fell in battle at the hands of his enemies.

Dr. Seward returns to his office at the asylum. One of his patients, Renfield, has lately been eating flies and spiders and talking out loud to an invisible "Master" who he believes is coming to help him. Seward finds Renfield lying face down in a pool of blood in his cell. The patient's back is broken and his face is bruised and bloody. Seward realizes that Dracula has been there to kill poor Renfield.

THE CHASE

The group rushes to Carfax Abbey, near Dr. Seward's asylum, to find and destroy the boxes of earth that Dracula calls home. They are determined to do away with the monster. But they leave Mina behind, alone and unguarded. While the group is away, Dracula takes the form of a thick mist and sneaks into Mina's room. While she sleeps, he materializes. He forces her to drink his blood.

Mina realizes that soon she, too, will be walking with the undead. When Van Helsing places a holy communion wafer on her forehead for protection, the wafer sears her flesh and leaves a scar. But the sickness has not yet transformed her. She will help Seward and Van Helsing trap Dracula.

Van Helsing hypnotizes Mina into a trance. She is gradually coming under Dracula's power, and her unconscious mind knows of Dracula's actions and sensations, no matter how far away he is. She hears sailors' voices and their footsteps on a wooden deck. She hears the clank of an anchor chain. Dracula must be on a ship. Fearing the hammer and stake that destroyed Lucy, he must be leaving England and sailing back home to Transylvania.

Van Helsing prepares the group for the journey to the Balkans. Before Dracula reaches his castle, they must stop him, drive a stake through his heart, and destroy him once and for all. Mina will guide them—in her hypnotic trances, she can hear what Dracula hears, sense what he senses.

The group retraces Jonathan Harker's journey across the continent to eastern Europe. They reach the coast of the Black Sea, where a ship unloads the vampire's coffin for the final trip to the castle. In her trance, Mina hears wolves howling, rough voices, and the lowing of cattle. Dracula's coffin has reached land. A band of armed Slovaks are escorting the Count upstream along a river.

Van Helsing's group splits up. Arthur Holmwood and Jonathan Harker will follow the Count in a small river steamboat. Quincey Morris and Dr. Seward saddle horses to chase the Slovaks by land. Van Helsing and Mina will take the trail over the Borgo Pass to Castle Dracula. Along the way, the professor will hypnotize Mina to follow Dracula's trail.

The nights are cold; snow begins to fall. Van Helsing and Mina climb the steep tracks into the high Carpathian Mountains. As she approaches Castle Dracula, Mina comes increasingly under Dracula's unseen power. She begins to sleep by day and lay awake by night. One terrifying night, in the shadow of Castle Dracula, the Count's three vampire women materialize near Mina. "Come sister. Come to us. Come! Come!" they plead. Mina recoils in horror. Van Helsing has used holy water to draw a ring around her. He repels the three vampires with a sacred wafer.

Leaving Mina in her sleep, Van Helsing climbs to the castle's gates. There he finds coffins and the bodies of the undead. He drives a stake through their hearts and destroys them one by one. He rejoins Mina and sets off down the track to meet Count Dracula.

Sunset is drawing near. Holmwood, Morris, Seward, and Harker have caught up with a band of gypsies who are now escorting Dracula's coffin. They draw their weapons and prepare for a fight. From behind a nearby rock, Van Helsing and Mina rise with their weapons aimed and ready. The gypsies carry knives and pistols. Harker and Morris force their way past them; one of them stabs Morris. Bleeding and staggering, he moves past them and helps Harker pry the lid from the coffin.

The Count is waking. Just as Dracula opens his blood-red eyes to greet the night, Harker shears off the monster's head with his knife. Quincey Morris drives his bowic knife through the Count's heart.

As the sun disappears behind the mountains, the scar left by the holy wafer disappears from Mina's head. The gypsies flee, and Quincey Morris falls to the ground. "God be thanked that all has not been in vain!" he says, dying. "The curse has passed away!"

Walpurgis-Nacht

189		MORNING.	EVENING.	REMARKS.
May 1	Monday	Dead House Harker leaves Munich 8.35 P.m.		
2	Tuesday	arrive Vienna 6.45 a.m. Leave Vienna 8.25 a.m.	Arrive Buda Pest 1.30 P.m. Leaves 2 P.m.	
3	Wednesday	Arrive Klausenburg 8 a.m. arrive Bistritz 8 P.m. Leaves Klausenburg Co. 34 P.m.		
4	Thursday	Leaves Bistritz 2 P.m. Leaves Bistritz 2 P.m. arrive Borgo Pass at 9 P.m. (an hour early)		
5	Friday	9 H drove to Castle		
6	Saturday	Castle		
May 7	Sunday	Castle Reason		
May 8	Monday	Castle a prison		
9	Tuesday	Castle letting loose		
10	Wednesday	Castle sees cat to cut of creature		
11	Thursday	Castle the woman kissing		
12	Friday	Castle takes out letter. Sees Count go out of Window		
13	Saturday	gypsies letter to gypsies - Count drawing		
May 14	Sunday			
May 15	Monday	Women kissing		
16	Tuesday			
17	Wednesday	Says letter to Mina		
18	Thursday			
19	Friday	Jonathan told to write letters		
20	Saturday			
May 21	Sunday			
May 22	Monday			
23	Tuesday			
24	Wednesday	Sees woman again		Says letter to Mina 3
25	Thursday	A memo to other		
26	Friday	Telegram Arthur to Quincey		
27	Saturday			
May 28	Sunday	Letter to gypsies Count discovers		

Stoker used a diary to plan the events of Dracula.

Chapter **SEVEN**

THE BOOK OF
THE UNDEAD

BRAM STOKER WORKED FOR SEVEN YEARS ON *Dracula*. Never before and never again would he spend so much time researching and writing a book. He took thousands of pages of notes from the guides, maps, and histories he studied. He worked up careful outlines of the novel, dividing it into three parts—like a play—and twenty-seven chapters. Using a one-year business diary, he marked each date with the events that were to take place in the book.

More than anything, Stoker wanted *Dracula* to settle his reputation as a writer. He wanted his readers and critics to admire the writing as well as the complicated plotting and structure. Instead of a traditional narrative, with one person describing the people and events, Stoker wrote *Dracula* as a series of "primary sources": diary entries, newspaper articles, reports, notes, letters, and transcriptions of phonograph recordings. There is no single point of view. Instead, different narrators give separate accounts of the strange events. Stoker borrowed this method from the English writer Wilkie Collins, who used it in a mystery story called *The Woman in White*.

Dracula was also Stoker's longest novel, running four hundred pages. Many of his friends and acquaintances appear in the book, disguised as fictional characters. Stoker took the name of Jonathan Harker from Joseph Harker, a set designer who worked for the Lyceum Theatre. Professor Van Helsing was based on Professor Arminius Vambéry. Many of Stoker's friends and critics believed that Count Dracula was a combination of two men: the historical Vlad Tepes and the most important man in Stoker's own life, Henry Irving.

The first edition of *Dracula* appeared in May 1897. The publisher, Constable, printed three thousand copies. The book had a yellow cover and red lettering and cost six shillings. Two years later, the first American edition was published by the firm of Doubleday & McClure. In 1901, Constable published a paperback edition, and *Dracula* had its first foreign translation— into Icelandic.

Dracula earned a few favorable reviews. Critics compared the story to Mary Shelley's *Frankenstein* and to the horror stories of Edgar Allan Poe. Stoker's own mother loved the book. "My dear, it is splendid," she wrote, "a thousand miles beyond anything you have written before, and I feel certain will place you very high in the writers of the day...."

In the meantime, Stoker had written a stage version of *Dracula* that ran four hours. It was performed only once, as a recital that took place just a few days before the book was published. The performance allowed Stoker to license his play, which protected him in case anyone should try to copy the characters and plot of his story. This performance won no reviews, except for a short comment from Henry Irving.

A page from Stoker's outline of Dracula

The building with columns is the Lyceum Theatre as it looked in the early1900s.

After hearing a bit of the play, Irving was asked his opinion, and answered, "Dreadful!"

Dracula did not enjoy the success Stoker had hoped for, and it did not make him very much money. He continued to work for Henry Irving, spending the next eight years in Irving's company and writing Gothic horror novels. But Stoker seemed to have spent all of his imagination and talent on *Dracula;* his later books were not as popular and not as good. With the same flowery language that he had used in *Dracula,* he tried to shock his readers with grotesque characters and events. At the same time, the Gothic novel went out of style. Audiences lost interest in ghosts, castles, women in distress, and the riddle of death.

In 1898, a fire destroyed the stage props and painted scenery at the Lyceum Theatre. Henry Irving suffered illness and an injury to his knee that forced him to cancel most of his performances. In 1905, Irving died in a London hotel. Stoker's career as a theatrical manager was over.

One of Stoker's last books was another vampire story called *Lady of the Shroud,* which came out in 1909. In 1910, he published a book called *Famous Imposters,* about people who had changed their identities. Stoker may have wanted to change his own—he was growing poor and had to apply to the government for financial help. In 1912, he died at his home in London at the age of sixty-four.

But *Dracula* lived on.

PART III

DRACULA ON STAGE AND SCREEN

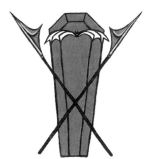

Chapter **EIGHT**

VAMPIRE SHOWS

OVER THE COURSE OF NEARLY FIVE HUNDRED years, Dracula has changed several times. He began in the fifteenth century as a sadistic but heroic Balkan prince. After his death, he became a legendary monster in the writings of German monks who had suffered under his reign. In the 1890s, Bram Stoker transformed Dracula into a vampire—a creature that survives after death by drinking the blood of the living.

Ten years after the death of Bram Stoker, an Irish theater manager named Hamilton Deane wrote his own stage version of *Dracula*. Deane had been a member of Henry Irving's theater company and had bought the rights to the story from Florence Stoker, Bram Stoker's widow. Before putting on the play, however,

Deane had to allow government censors to read it. None of them appreciated *Dracula:* "I thought the novel tedious rubbish," said one. "The play is also rubbish, of course, but the details of it seem to me too disgusting for the stage." The censors allowed the show to go on anyway.

Deane's version of *Dracula* opened in June 1924 at the Grand Theatre in Derby, England. Deane himself played Dr. Van Helsing, and the actor Edmund Blake played Count Dracula. Despite the censors' opinions, the production proved to be a smash hit. Deane planned to bring the play to London, but theatrical producers in the big city weren't interested. London audiences, they believed, were too sophisticated to take an interest in an old-fashioned ghost story.

Deane himself had to pay for the production, which opened on Valentine's Day, 1927, at the Little Theatre. Raymond Huntley played Dracula in a new costume Deane had created for the Count: an elegant black tuxedo with a long black cape. At one point in the play, Dracula swirled the cape around his head, dropped through a trap door, and disappeared from the stage. As an added frightening touch, Deane hired a professional nurse to stand by to assist audience members who might faint.

While the London critics gave *Dracula* poor reviews, audiences loved it. Hamilton Deane's production ran for a grand total of 391 performances. An American producer, Horace Liveright, saw the play and hired a journalist named John Balderston to adapt it for a production on Broadway, in New York. Balderston simplified the story, cutting out the characters of Quincey Morris and Arthur Holmwood, and producers carefully screened several actors for the part of Count Dracula. In late July 1927, they called a Hungarian actor named Bela Lugosi to the stage to read for the part of the vampire.

"I . . . AM DRACULA"

Bela Lugosi was a struggling Hungarian actor who had been in the United States for only a few years. He was born Béla Blasko in the Transylvanian town of Lugos in 1882. (When Lugosi was growing up, Lugos and Transylvania belonged to Hungary. Now Lugos lies within the borders of Romania.) As a young man, Lugosi trained to be a locksmith. But he didn't have much enthusiasm for the job, and before his career as a locksmith began, he moved to Szeged, Hungary, to join the Varosi Szinhaz, a repertory theater company (a group that performs several different plays during a season). He played Romeo in William Shakespeare's *Romeo and Juliet*. "He is a man and in love when he plays a man and a lover," said one critic after seeing the play. "Wild, violent in love, and his aching heart almost breaking when as Romeo he sees his beautiful Juliet dead." In 1913 Lugosi joined the National Theater of Hungary, where he played in Shakespeare's *Hamlet*.

Bela Lugosi, left, *plays a villain in* The Silent Command.

In 1914, when World War I broke out, Lugosi joined the Hungarian army. He fought for a year and a half in Serbia and Russia and was wounded twice. After he left the army, he began acting in films. He made several movies with the talented Hungarian director Mihaly Kertesz. (Later, Kertesz moved to Hollywood, changed his name to Michael Curtiz, and directed the film *Casablanca.*) Lugosi played the lead character in the Hungarian film of *The Picture of Dorian Gray,* which was released in 1918.

In the next year, after the end of World War I, a Communist revolution swept through Hungary. Lugosi joined a left-wing actor's union and played a prominent role in a time of violent political conflict. When Hungary's revolutionary leaders were overthrown, he moved to Germany to escape imprisonment and a possible death sentence for his political activities. In Berlin, he searched desperately for some way to support himself. Fortunately, films did not yet demand speech—only movement and emphatic gestures. Lugosi acted in a film directed by F. W. Murnau called *The Janus Head,* based on the story of Dr. Jekyll and Mr. Hyde. He also played an American Indian in *Leatherstocking,* based on the stories of James Fenimore Cooper.

Still poor and struggling, Lugosi saw the cloud of revolution and violence descend on Germany as it had on Hungary. He took a ship to the United States. Once there, he hired a tutor to teach him English, began acting in Hungarian plays in New York, and landed a small role in a play called *The Red Poppy.* He then moved to Hollywood, where he made his first American film, *The Silent Command,* in 1923. In this movie, he plays a tall, elegant villain.

Lugosi acted in many silent films that have long since been forgotten, including *The Midnight Girl, The Thirteenth Chair,* and *Wild Company.* After a few years in Hollywood, Lugosi returned to New York. Although he could make enough money in Hollywood to live, his real home was the stage.

In July 1927, Lugosi auditioned for the part of Count Dracula in John Balderston's version of the play. Balderston and producer Horace Liveright were quite taken with Lugosi's appearance and stage presence. They also liked his strong Hungarian accent, which seemed just right for the part of the Count. Lugosi got the job.

The Broadway production of *Dracula* ran for 261 performances. After the play closed in New York, it moved to the Biltmore Theater in Los Angeles. Bela Lugosi again played the lead, this time for audiences that included Hollywood's leading film producers and directors. The play's success both in New York and Los Angeles led several movie studios to consider buying the rights to the story and filming it.

One serious problem stood in the way: movies were still silent. Somehow, the history and mythology of vampires, which were unfamiliar to many Americans, would have to be explained. To do this, a silent film of *Dracula* would have to use long, complicated title cards. Reading the cards, the audience would quickly lose interest in the action.

One silent movie of the Dracula story had already been made in Germany. *Nosferatu*, directed by F. W. Murnau, had transformed Dracula into the evil Count Orlok (played by Max Schreck), a strange creature with long, pointed ears and grotesque fingernails. Murnau's film was popular with critics, who saw it as a work of surrealist or expressionist cinema. But Murnau had made one serious mistake. He thought he only had to credit Stoker in the title of the film and change Dracula's name to avoid buying the rights to the story. Florence Stoker quickly sued the director and the studio that had produced *Nosferatu*. She won the lawsuit. Most of the copies of the film were burned and the studio went bankrupt.

By the late 1920s, as sound films began appearing, other movie studios were preparing new versions of *Dracula*. In the United States, Universal Studios bought the rights to the story in August 1930 for forty thousand dollars. A writer named Dudley Murphy wrote a screenplay based on the novel. The studio hired Tod Browning to direct the movie and Bela Lugosi for the starring role. Lugosi's halting, accented English seemed perfect for the part, right from his very first line in the movie's script: "I . . . am Dracula."

In 1931, *Dracula* was transformed once again, this time by a Hungarian actor who could barely speak English. (Some writers believe that Lugosi wasn't sure

Bela Lugosi portrayed Dracula in a sinister cape.

of the meaning of his lines—which accounted for his strange, halting speech.) It was Lugosi who gave Count Dracula his most familiar face and voice, the one we all imagine when anyone mentions Dracula's name. He had a pale face, staring eyes, heavy eyebrows, a sharp nose, and black hair combed back from the top of his head. Lugosi's Dracula wore the fine tuxedo and black cape introduced by Hamilton Deane. He spoke with a heavy accent and moved from room to room quickly and silently.

The movie of *Dracula* made several important changes to Bram Stoker's story. At the beginning of

Promotional posters for Dracula *were very dramatic.*

CARL LAEMMLE presents

DRACULA

UNIVERSAL PICTURE

the story it is Renfield, not Jonathan Harker, who goes to Castle Dracula. Renfield's encounter with the vampire turns him into a raving lunatic. Mina Murray becomes Mina Seward, the daughter of Dr. John Seward. Lucy Westenra is renamed Lucy Weston. After Dracula bites her, she dies immediately—there are no blood transfusions. Professor Van Helsing lives on to do battle with Dracula in London, but Quincey Morris and Arthur Holmwood disappear altogether from the story.

Dracula was a hit. It was first shown in New York in February 1931 and became the most profitable film for Universal Studios that year. Audiences filled movie theaters to experience a new cinematic sensation: fear of the supernatural. The heads of the studio knew that other productions of the Dracula story would also be a success. They began to plan new productions, not only of the Dracula story but of other Gothic horror tales such as *Frankenstein, The Mummy,* and *The Invisible Man.* For a few years, horror films were all the rage in Hollywood.

FAME AND MISFORTUNE

The success of *Dracula* made Lugosi an international movie star. Women, in particular, had been fascinated by him ever since he played the Count on Broadway. "Women wrote me letters," Lugosi once said, "Ah, what letters women wrote me! Young girls. Women from seventeen to thirty. Letters of a horrible hunger.

Asking me if I cared only for maiden's blood. Asking me if I had done the play because I was in reality that sort of *thing*. . . . It made me know that the women of America are unsatisfied, famished, craving sensation, even though it be the sensation of death draining the red blood of life."

Yet Lugosi, and many film critics, were disappointed by the movie version of *Dracula*. The opening scenes in Dracula's castle were spooky and realistic. But beginning with the scene of Renfield's return to London, when Dr. Seward and Van Helsing begin their battle with the Count, the film slowed down. Instead of a suspenseful horror story, it became a talky and static film version of a stage production. Worse, the chase scene in the Transylvanian wilds at the end of Bram Stoker's novel was cut, replaced by a tame ending that takes place in England.

Lugosi already had a low opinion of Hollywood films, which he believed turned classic stories into lightweight entertainment. After all, he had acted in Shakespeare's plays. He had sung in musicals and had been one of the biggest theater stars in Hungary. Now he was nothing more than Hollywood's best-known horror character. Shortly after *Dracula* was made, Universal offered him the part of Dr. Frankenstein's monster, a dead criminal brought back to life by Dr. Frankenstein, in a film adaptation of Mary Shelley's novel. The monster would have to wear heavy makeup through long working days. He would have no lines to speak—he would only grunt, gesture, scream, and kill. To Bela Lugosi, the role seemed demeaning. He turned it down. The studio chose instead a British actor named Boris Karloff, and soon another horror star was born in Hollywood.

During the 1930s, Universal Studios followed up the success of *Dracula* and *Frankenstein* with many more horror films. But for Lugosi, *Dracula* proved to be the first and last success of his entire movie career. He still had trouble using English; his thick accent and his fame as Dracula typecast him, making it difficult for Hollywood studios to see him in any other role. For several years, Lugosi could find no work at all in Hollywood.

Gloria Holden as Dracula's daughter

Chapter NINE

DRACULA IN HOLLYWOOD

THE **DRACULA** FAMILY OF MOVIES GREW IN THE 1930s and 1940s. In 1936, five years after Tod Browning's *Dracula* was released, Universal made *Dracula's Daughter*—which many critics believe is a better film. In 1943, the studio made *Son of Dracula,* a sequel to the original *Dracula.* But instead of casting Bela Lugosi in the starring role, the studio chose Lon Chaney Jr., who had already played the Wolfman. Chaney cut a very different figure from Lugosi on the screen. He was taller and heavier; his face wore a sad, stony expression. His movements were awkward, and—worst of all—he had no accent.

Since Stoker had written only one book about Count Dracula, movie studios had to keep changing the plot and inventing new characters to create something new and interesting for audiences. The story changed a little more in *Horror of Dracula,* a British movie that appeared in 1958 and that was the first to film the Dracula story in color. At the start of *Horror of Dracula,* it is Professor Van Helsing (played by Peter Cushing) who goes to Dracula's castle. Instead of a gloomy, dark ruin, the castle is a fine old mansion, with pretty tapestries, marble floors, and splendid suits of armor. Van Helsing finds that Jonathan Harker has already been killed by Dracula (played by Christopher Lee). At the end of the film, Van Helsing bests the Count by opening the curtains and destroying the vampire with the light of day. Dracula struggles against the light, but slowly turns into a gruesome pile of skin, bones, and dust, which blows away as the film credits roll.

Although it further changed Bram Stoker's story, *Horror of Dracula* turned out to be a good film, with fine performances by Christopher Lee and Peter Cushing. The studio spent large sums of money on the well-made sets, costumes, and props. The director used quick cuts to keep the suspense high as the film moved from one scene to the next. Hammer Films went on to make many more horror movies, several of them starring Lee as Count Dracula.

By the 1950s, Dracula and vampires had become common themes in movies and books. The story turned western in an American film called *Curse of the Undead.* In this film, the vampire changes from a

European count into a black-hatted gunfighter named Drake Robey. Later, another Dracula western appeared called *Billy the Kid Versus Dracula.*

But while these new Dracula films were being written and filmed, Bela Lugosi was acting in poorly written, low-budget productions. He played mad doctors, evil aristocrats, and, in one film, a scientist who turns into a werewolf. In many films, his costume remained the same: a dark suit and a long black cape.

In the late 1940s, Lugosi played Dracula again in a comedy called *Abbott and Costello Meet Frankenstein.* The three biggest Universal horror stars—Lugosi, Boris Karloff, and Lon Chaney Jr.—starred in the

Abbott and Costello met more than just Frankenstein in their monster movie.

movie. By now, horror figures were familiar to everyone. The actors had become cartoon figures chasing the comedy team of Abbott and Costello around castle rooms and through misty swamps. The movie was not very funny and not very frightening.

Although Lugosi was proud of the fame and recognition he earned from *Dracula,* he was growing very bitter about the Hollywood film industry. He had made only $3,500 for the seven weeks he worked on the film, while the studio had made millions. After *Dracula,* directors and movie producers ignored him or cast him in dreadful low-budget movies, while Lugosi slipped deeper and deeper into poverty. Sometime in the 1940s, he became addicted to morphine, a powerful drug used as a painkiller. Desperate to be cured, he checked himself into a hospital for treatment. When he left the clinic after three months he was much healthier, but he had only a short time to live.

In 1955, a director named Edward D. Wood Jr. asked Lugosi to play a part in a film called *The Bride of the Monster.* Needing a star and with very little money to shoot the film, Wood turned to Lugosi. His name was still well known, but he would work for very little money. *The Bride of the Monster* flopped, but in the next year, Wood asked Lugosi to act in another of his movies, *Plan 9 from Outer Space.* A few of Lugosi's scenes were completed. But just a few days after the crew began shooting the film, the actor collapsed and died at his home.

Instead of writing Lugosi's character out of the film, Wood simply hired a double to play in the rest of Lugosi's scenes. Wearing the famous black cape, the replacement stalked around with the cape drawn over the bottom half of his face—not to scare the audience, but to disguise himself. *Plan 9 from Outer Space* was supposed to be a combination of science fiction and horror. The movie showed hostile aliens arriving from outer space to bring ghouls and demons out of their graves and hiding places. The film was a complete disaster and was once voted "Worst Film Ever Made." Most people who have seen it agree. It was a sad end to Bela Lugosi's career as a film actor.

Grandpa, left, and Eddie Munster showed that vampires could be funny.

Chapter **TEN**

THE MODERN DRACULA

BRAM STOKER'S **DRACULA** HAS INSPIRED MANY modern writers to create their own version of the classic vampire tale. Although the Gothic novel faded away at the beginning of the twentieth century, vampires survived in comic books, inexpensive "pulp" magazines, short stories, and movies. Even the old stage play of *Dracula* came back to life in the 1970s, when it was turned into a successful Broadway production.

But for many years after World War II, the science fiction genre was much more popular than horror. The real-life stories of American and Russian space missions made science fiction much more believable than old tales of the occult. Outer space held its own adventures and mysteries. Scientists became the new heroes, and their inventions were the new realm of cinema drama and suspense.

But in the 1960s, the public began taking interest in superstition and the occult again. New Dracula movies were made, including *The Fearless Vampire Killers* in 1967. The vampire even made it to television in the comedy *The Munsters*. In this show, Grandpa wears a long black cape, while young Eddie sports the classic Count Dracula hairstyle.

THE VAMPIRE CHRONICLERS

Many authors have borrowed from the Count Dracula figure to create their own versions of the vampire myth. *Salem's Lot,* a novel by Stephen King, moved Bram Stoker's story from England to a small town in Maine. In the 1970s, a young writer named Anne Rice created her own family of vampires. "I was just sitting at the typewriter," she explained, "wondering what it would be like if a vampire told you the truth about what it was like to be a vampire. I wanted to know what it really feels like."

In her book *Interview with the Vampire,* a vampire named Louis tells his story to a boy, who records the interview on a cassette tape player. Louis has been a member of the undead since the 1790s, when he was first attacked by a vampire named Lestat. The author describes Louis as "utterly white and smooth, as if he were sculpted from bleached bone, and his face was as seemingly inanimate as a statue, except for two brilliant green eyes that looked down at the boy intently like flames in a skull."

Lestat instructs Louis on what it is like to be a vampire. Louis, in turn, tells the boy all that he knows. He contradicts much of the classic vampire myth. He enjoys looking at crucifixes, instead of being afraid of them. A stake through the heart would not destroy him. And as much as he'd like to, he cannot pass from place to place as a cloud of mist.

Louis and Lestat were a new interpretation of the vampire first described by Bram Stoker. But unlike *Dracula*, Rice's *Interview with the Vampire* turned out to be an instant best-seller. She wrote four more vampire books about Lestat, calling the whole series "The Vampire Chronicles." In 1994, the first story was turned into a movie, starring Tom Cruise as Lestat.

DRACULA LIVES

Everyone seems to know who Count Dracula is, but hardly anyone is afraid of him anymore. One important reason is his familiarity. Count Dracula no longer seems very strange—in fact, he is often portrayed as friendly. A bit dangerous perhaps, but never boring.

In the 1990s, vampires have turned up in advertisements, in movies, on cereal boxes, and even on *Sesame Street*, where a purple-faced Count helps young viewers learn about numbers. Every Halloween, trick-or-treaters put on long black capes and plastic fangs to bite each other in the neck. People with an

A vampire puppet called The Count teaches children about numbers on Sesame Street®.

interest in the occult and black magic have formed clubs to celebrate Dracula, Vlad Tepes, and Bram Stoker. Dracula even has his own Internet newsgroups and World Wide Web sites.

Meanwhile, in Romania and Transylvania, many people still believe in vampires. However, very few Romanians associate the historical Vlad Tepes, Prince Dracula, with this superstition. Instead, Vlad Tepes is a hero, especially in the Wallachian area of Romania, for defending his nation against the Ottoman Empire. A monument to Vlad Tepes stands in Tirgoviste. Other statues and busts of Dracula can be seen in the towns of Wallachia, where thousands of tourists arrive every year to visit the ruins of Castle Dracula, the palace of Tirgoviste, and other places associated with the prince. In 1976, during the five hundredth anniversary year of Vlad's death, the Romanian government even issued a stamp in his honor.

Your opinion of Dracula depends on who you are, what you see and read, and where you live. But the fascination with Dracula goes deeper than a scary old count with fangs. Deep down, this fascination is the fear, and the eagerness, we have about what happens after the final chapter is written and we join the many others who already know what it is like to pass from the land of the living. There's still a chance that we might meet a tall, dark-caped figure.

As Professor Van Helsing once said: "When you get home tonight and the lights have been turned out and you are afraid to look behind the curtains and you dread to see a face appear at the window—why, just pull yourself together and remember that after all there are such things!"

SOURCES

12–13   Raymond T. McNally and Radu Florescu, *In Search of Dracula* (New York: Houghton Mifflin, 1994), 54.

38–39   McNally and Florescu, 79.

47   Basil Copper, *The Vampire in Legend, Fact, and Art* (Secaucus, NJ: The Citadel Press, 1974), 45.

59   Leonard Wolf, *Dracula: The Connoisseur's Guide* (New York: Broadway Books, 1997), 22–23.

62   Raymond T. McNally and Radu Florescu, *The Essential Dracula* (New York: Mayflower Books, 1979), 69.

64   Bram Stoker, *Dracula* (New York: The Modern Library, n.d.), 17.

64–65   Ibid., 23.

65   Ibid., 43.

66   McNally, *The Essential Dracula*, 101.

69   Stoker, *Dracula*, 188.

70   Ibid., 232.

70–71   Ibid., 237.

71   McNally, *The Essential Dracula*, 175.

72   Stoker, *Dracula*, 246.

74   Ibid., 406.

75   Ibid., 417.

79   Ibid., 274.

80   Ibid., 270.

84   Ibid., 328.

85   Arthur Lennig, *The Count: The Life and Films of Bela "Dracula" Lugosi* (New York: G. P. Putnam's Sons, 1974), 34.

91–92   Ibid., 71.

102   Katherine Ramsland, *The Vampire Companion* (New York: Ballantine Books, 1993), 195.

102–103   Anne Rice, *Interview with the Vampire* (New York: Ballantine Books, 1977), 4.

105   Stoker, *Dracula*, 417.

BIBLIOGRAPHY

Belford, Barbara. *Bram Stoker: A Biography of the Author of Dracula*. New York: Alfred A. Knopf, 1996.

Copper, Basil. *The Vampire in Legend, Fact, and Art*. Secaucus, NJ: The Citadel Press, 1974.

Fossier, Robert, ed. *The Cambridge Illustrated History of the Middle Ages, 1250-1520*. Cambridge: Cambridge University Press, 1986.

Hart, James V., and Fred Saberhagen. *Bram Stoker's Dracula: The Novel of the Film Directed by Francis Ford Coppola*. New York: The Signet Group, 1992.

Lennig, Arthur. *The Count: The Life and Films of Bela "Dracula" Lugosi*. New York: G. P. Putnam's Sons, 1974.

McNally, Raymond T., and Radu Florescu. *In Search of Dracula*. New York: Houghton Mifflin Company, 1994.

Ramsland, Katherine. *The Vampire Companion*. New York: Ballantine Books, 1993.

Rice, Anne. *Interview with the Vampire*. New York: Ballantine Books, 1977.

Stoker, Bram. *Dracula*. New York: The Modern Library, n.d.

Wolf, Leonard. *Dracula: The Connoisseur's Guide*. New York: Broadway Books, 1997.

Wolf, Leonard, ed. *The Essential Dracula: The Definitive Annotated Edition of Bram Stoker's Classic Novel*. New York: Plume, 1993.

FILMOGRAPHY

Nosferatu
Prana Films
Directed by F. W. Murnau
Starring Max Schreck as Count
    Orlok
Released 1922

Dracula
Universal Studios
Directed by Tod Browning
Starring Bela Lugosi as Count
    Dracula
Released 1931

Dracula's Daughter
Universal Studios
Directed by Lambert Hillyer
Staring Gloria Holden
Released 1936

Son of Dracula
Universal Studios
Directed by Robert Siodmak
Starring Lon Chaney Jr. as
    Count Alucard
Released 1943

The Horror of Dracula
Hammer Films (England)
Directed by Terence Fisher
Starring Christopher Lee as
    Count Dracula
Released 1958

Billy the Kid Versus Dracula
Circle Productions
Directed by William Beaudine
Starring John Carradine as
    Count Dracula
Released 1965

Blacula
American International
    Pictures
Directed by William Crane
Starring William Marshall as
    Blacula
Released 1972

Nosferatu
Gaumont (Germany)
Directed by Werner Herzog
Starring Klaus Kinski as Count
    Dracula
Released 1979

Bram Stoker's Dracula
Zoetrope Studios
Directed by Francis Ford
    Coppola
Starring Gary Oldman as
    Count Dracula
Released 1992

Interview with the Vampire
Warner Brothers
Directed by Neil Jordon
Starring Tom Cruise as Lestat
Released 1994

Ed Wood
Touchstone Pictures
Directed by Tim Burton
Starring Martin Landau as
    Bela Lugosi
Released 1994

INDEX

Abbott and Costello Meet Frankenstein, 97–98

Balcombe, Florence. *See* Stoker, Florence
Balderston, John, 85, 87
Bathory, Elizabeth, 48
Billy the Kid Versus Dracula, 97
boyars, 16, 24, 25, 30, 33, 35, 37
Bride of the Monster, The, 98
Byron, Lord, 49

Carmilla, 51
Carpathian Mountains, 6, 11, 32–33
Chaney Jr., Lon, 95
Christian Europe, 16–18, 29–30
Constantinople, 11, 23, 30. *See also* Istanbul
corpses, valley of, 10–12
Corvinus, Matthias, 32, 35–37
"Crystal Cup, The," 56
Curse of the Undead, 96–97

Danesti, 16, 18, 30
Deane, Hamilton, 83–84, 90
death, mystery of, 41–42
Doyle, Sir Arthur Conan, 51
Dracula: book, 6, 57, 63–75, 77–78; movie (1931), 7, 89–91, 92, 98; stage versions, 79–80, 83–85, 88, 101

Dracula, Count, "The Count" (character), 6–7, 61, 84, 89–90, 103–105
Dracula's Daughter, 95

Famous Impostors, 81
Fearless Vampire Killers, The, 102
Frankenstein, 49, 78, 92–93

Gerard, Emily, 58–59
Gothic novels, 48–51, 54, 80

Haigh, John, 48
hematomania, 48
Holmes, Sherlock, 51
Holy Roman Empire, 17–18
Horror of Dracula, 96
Hungary, 16, 18, 24, 30, 32, 36
Hunyadi, John, 20–21, 22, 24

impalement, 10, 24, 28, 31, 33
Interview with the Vampire, 102–103
Irving, Henry, 55, 56–57, 79–81, 83
Istanbul, 10, 11, 13, 31. See also Constantinople

King, Stephen, 102

Lady of the Shroud, 81
Land Beyond the Forest, The, 58–59

Le Fanu, Joseph Sheridan, 51
Liveright, Horace, 84–85, 87
Lugosi, Bela, 7, 85–93, 97–99
Lyceum Theatre, 56–57, 81

Medeugna, 45–47
Mircea, 15, 21
Mohammed II, 9–13, 23,
    32–33
Moldavia, 15, 21
Munsters, The, 102
Murad II, 18–20
Murnau, F.W., 88
Murphy, Dudley, 89

Nosferatu, 88

Order of the Dragon, 18
Ottoman Empire, 9–11,
    16–18, 20, 29–32

Picture of Dorian Gray, The,
    51
Plan 9 From Outer Space,
    98–99
Poele, Arnold, 46–47
Polidori, John, 49–50

Radu the Handsome, 15, 20,
    21, 33, 35, 36, 37
Rice, Anne, 102–103
Rivals, The, 55
Rymer, James Malcolm, 50

Salem's Lot, 102
Saxons, 27–29
Shelley, Mary Wollstonecraft,
    49, 78, 92
Snake's Pass, The, 57

Son of Dracula, 95
Stevenson, Robert Louis, 51
Stoker, Bram, 6, 39, 51; as
    business manager, 56–57,
    80–81; childhood of, 53;
    civil-service career of, 54;
    learning about Dracula,
    57–61, 77; published works
    by, 56, 57, 78–81; in Whitby,
    England, 60–61. *See also*
    Dracula
Stoker, Florence, 56, 83,
    88–89
*Strange Case of Dr. Jekyll and
    Mr. Hyde, The,* 51, 87
superstitions, 41; vampire,
    43–45
Sussex Vampire, The, 51

Tirgoviste, 10, 28–29, 32–33,
    35; palace at, 25, 31, 104
Transylvania, 6, 9–10, 12–13,
    15–18, 24, 27, 32, 35, 37;
    books about, 58–59
Turks, 9–11, 15–18, 20–23,
    30–37

Under the Sunset, 51

Vambéry, Arminius, 58
vampire: becoming a, 43–44;
    books about, 6, 49–51,
    63–75, 81, 102–103;
    destroying a, 45, 51, 59;
    finding a, 45; forms of a,
    44; of Medeugna, 45–47;
    modern, 103–105; movies
    about, 88–92, 95–99, 102,
    103; origin of name, 42;

protection against, 45;
superstitions, 43–45
vampire panics, 45–47
*Varney the Vampire or The
Feast of Blood*, 50
Vlad II (Dracul), 15–21, 30
Vlad III (Dracula), 7; battling
Saxons, 27–29; battling
Turks, 9–13, 29–35; birth of,
15; books based on, 63–75;
death of, 37; Hunyadi
influence on, 22; legend of,
38–39, 104–105; as Prince

of Wallachia, 21, 24, 37; as
prisoner, 20–21, 35–37;
reputation of, 6, 24–25,
28–29; and use of torture,
10, 24–25, 28–29, 31, 33,
38–39
Vladislav II, 21, 24, 30

Wallachia, 6, 9–12, 16–21,
24–25, 27–29, 32–33, 35, 37
Wilde, Oscar, 51
Wilkinson, William, 61
Wood Jr., Edward D., 98–99

PRONUNCIATION GUIDE

Arges River	AHR-gesh
boyars	boh-YARS
Brasov	brah-SHOHV
Bucharest	BOO-kuh-rest
Buda	BOO-duh
Hunyadi, John	HOON-yaw-dee
janissaries	JAN-uh-sehr-eez
lamia	LAY-mee-uh
Lugos, Transylvania	LOO-gōzh
Lyceum Theatre	lye-SEE-uhm
Polidori, John	PAH-lee-DOR-ee
shish kebab	SHISH-kuh-bob
Sibiu, Transylvania	see-BEE-oo
Snagov, Romania	SNAH-gohv
Szeged, Hungary	SEH-ged
Tepes, Vlad	TSEH-pesh
Tirgoviste, Wallachia	tir-GO-veesh-teh
Transylvania	tran-suhl-VAY-nyuh
vrukalakos	vroo-kah-LAH-kos
Wallachia	wah-LAY-kee-uh

ABOUT THE AUTHOR

Tom Streissguth was born in Washington, D.C. He grew up in Minneapolis, where he watched a lot of horror movies and liked to dress up as a ghost on Halloween. After studying music at Yale University, Tom spent several years in Europe, where he lived about 300 miles from Castle Dracula. He has written more than 25 books for young people, including biographies of Willa Cather, Mary Cassatt, and Irving Berlin. He now lives with his family in Florida.

PHOTO ACKNOWLEDGMENTS

Corbis-Bettmann, 2, 12, 44, 55, 89; North Wind Picture Archive, 11, 23, 31, 49; IPS, 14; Fortean Picture Library, 26, 50, 60; © Simon Marsden/The Marsden Archive, 34, 36, 39; UPI/Corbis-Bettmann, 52; Shakespeare Centre Library, Stratford-Upon-Avon, 59; Mary Evans Picture Library/Tony Grubhofer, 80; Rosenbach Museum and Library, Philadelphia, PA, 76, 79; Archive Photos, 86, 90; Photofest, 94, 104; Universal Pictures/Archive Photos, 97; Hollywood Book and Poster, 100.

Front Cover: Corbis/Bettmann
Back Cover: Kunsthistorisches Museum, Vienna
Illustrations on pages 8, 40, 62, 66, 71, and 82 by John Erste
Map on page 19 by Laura Westlund